Quantum Attitude

SEO On A Zero Budget

By

Glenn Blake

DEDICATION

To all those who have spent countless hours fishing in the giant pond we call the internet! And to the people who have supported my workshops and events over the years.

CONTENTS

ACKNOWLEDGMENTS

I would like to acknowledge all the people who have helped me to bring this book to a reality.

FORWARD

The Quantum Attitude SEO On A Zero Budget book is not a get rich quick scheme or method that promises to make you an internet billionaire overnight. It has been developed using time tested methods that have been proven to improve your likelihood of succeeding online. I have used and taught the methods described in the following pages and can attest to the fact that they are quite effective and can be done on a zero budget!

A few short years ago it was common for potential clients to ask me "Why do I need a website?" Now this question is almost nonexistent! Without a strong web presence you are surely destined to fail in today's marketplace! With several of the major retailers making decisions to close their brick and mortar stores going completely online it is clearly apparent as to what direction the markets are going. It is now essential for any business to have a strong web presence. When we hear of a new business now we go home and look them up on the web.

The 2010 holiday shopping period was a major wakeup call to many retailers. Although the economy was in a deep recession holiday sales increased by 15 percent overall over the previous year. If we break the statistics down to online sales as opposed to standard brick and mortar sales the figures are staggering. Online sales accounted for over 73 percent of the sales! The message there is very clear, that more and more shoppers are taking advantage of online discounts and shopping from the comfort of their own home. The hustle and bustle at the retailers and malls across the world has been replaced by the low pressure ability to shop online. Less driving, no crowds to deal with and wider selections combined with very competitive pricing online has now changed the way the game is being played!

Over the last fifteen years I have watched the internet change and grow at an amazing rate. Although these changes come almost faster than you can keep up with them, the principles of search engine optimization remain the same. I have been successful in placing hundreds of websites in top positions on the search engines without fail. I have spent the last five years lecturing and teaching internet marketing and search engine optimization to audiences all around the world. I was also featured in the documentary Pass It On as a search engine expert! The methods I will share with you in the following pages have been proven over time and will definitely improve your search engine ranking. Although the internet is an ever changing environment the basic principle of how it works remains the same, you enter a query which is passed to a database and that database returns results based on the query. If you know what word format that the database requires for a particular result it is then much easier to control the results returned by the database. Controlling those results are essential to coming up at the top of the search engine listings. In 2005 I wrote the USC Database System which is now widely used online. The database was licensed to several major companies and was soon found to be efficient in presenting excellent results that could be filtered in a way that had not yet been accomplished. My knowledge and understanding of database principles soon allowed me to control other databases and search engines as well as my own. A few years ago this control was sufficient to keep a site high in the search results but as the internet has evolved there are other factors that must also be utilized in order to succeed online. Social networking, video marketing and link marketing are also an important part of strengthening your online presence. Your position in the search rankings is dependent on the way you design your site. Our goal in writing this book is to give you the edge and will do so every time following the directions given.

This book is written for the novice although most other users will find some interesting tips as well. Please bear in mind that I will take the time to explain certain terminology that some of you already know the meaning of. This is for those who do not understand the terminology!

Glenn Blake

KEYWORDS

One of the most important things to do is to select the correct keywords or key phrase. For those of you who do not understand what a keyword or key phrase is I will explain: a keyword or key phrase is what a user would normally type into a search engine in order to find a website offering the products or services that you have. In other words if you were to go online looking to buy a red hat you would type in red hat or hat. This keyword or key phrase could be any word or phrase that describes the product or service being offered.

Keyword selection is something that you should spend a bit of time on as the correct keyword or phrase is imperative. Do not assume that what you think they are typing is what you would type in. Take a look at several of your competitor's websites and view what keywords or phrases they are using. This can usually be done by going to their website and viewing the source code. For those of you who do not know how to do this you can simply go to the website that you want to research and on a Windows machine right click and choose view source or view page source depending on which browser you are using. On machines that do not utilize right clicking you can always find a tab on the browser that says "view", simply click there and choose view source or view page source. Once you do this pay particular attention to the line: <meta name="keywords" content="keywor1, keyword2, keyword3, keyword4, keyword5,">. Of course "keyword1 etc. will be replaced with the actual keywords or key phrases being used.

Another way to research keywords is to go online and search for something like "most used search terms". I am not in this book going to refer the reader to any particular site as sites like this come and go. If you do a search for them it would be more accurate for you than my recommending a certain site and by the time you read this book that site or web address is no longer accurate.

When selecting your keywords it is usually good to start out with about five keywords or key phrases. I will explain why in just a few more pages.

META TAGS

In the last few years I have heard several seo gurus say that your meta tags are no longer relevant to your search engine listings. Simply put, although the way search engines look at your tags varies, without them you could not be indexed properly! Your meta tags are what the search engines use to reference and index your site. The following example is a format that I have used and been very successful in:

```
<!DOCTYPE HTML PUBLIC "-//W3C//DTD HTML 4.0 Transitional//EN">
<HTML>
<HEAD>
<title>SEO On A Zero Budget</title>
<meta name="description"content=" SEO On A Zero Budget everything you need to succeed online.">
<meta name="keywords" content=" SEO On A Zero Budget,  seo, web design,  seo eBook,">
<META name="expires" content="no">
<META name="language" content="english, EN">
<META name="email" content="sales@yoursite.com">
<META name="publisher" content=" SEO On A Zero Budget ">
<META name=author content="Quantum Attitude">
<META name=copyright content="1996-2011 Quantum Attitude">
<META name=revisit-after content="3 days">
<META name=distribution content="Global">
<META name="robots" content="INDEX, FOLLOW">
<meta name=rating content="general">
<meta http-equiv="Content-Type" content="text/html; charset=iso-8859-1">
</head>
```

A few things to notice and keep in mind here; NEVER PUT YOUR REAL EMAIL ADDRESS IN THE EMAIL LINE UNLESS YOU ENJOY GETTING A LOT OF SPAM. This is one of the easiest places for spammers to get your email address.

The title line is important as well. Always put your primary keyword first (I will explain this in a few pages as well.) The title of your website should be no more that 60 characters including spaces.

The next line that I want you to pay attention to is the description line. This description should also start with your primary keyword or key phrase and the description should be no more that 150 characters including spaces.

Next we look at the keyword line. In the keyword content you must start with your primary keyword or phrase also. You can use 500 keywords here as I have seen many people do however I do not suggest it. For the novice about five or six should suffice.

The other lines in the meta tag format are pretty much self explanatory except for the revisit line. When you are in the process of building your site you should set this at a low number however once completed setting it at 7 days should be good.

You should when adding keywords to your meta tags not repeat the same word more than five times. I like to stick to the rule of not repeating keywords more than three times myself. Also the use of the words "search engine" should never be used!

The publisher and copyright lines should be filled out with the correct information as well as making sure that the content line is correct. One good point to remember is the rating content line. If you are servicing a global market then it should state global of course, however if you are offering a service that is locally based you will want to put in a state abbreviation code there. It makes no sense whatsoever to offer your yard maintenance service to someone in another country. By setting this to a state abbreviation it will help you with the localized search as well. The use of your meta tags as I have just explained is the first step in improving your over all search engine exposure and positioning.

PAGE DESIGN

Designing your website should be done in such a manner that your website loads in the user's browser in a reasonable amount of time. Search engines as well as visitors to your site are as a rule not impressed by a page that takes five minutes to load. They will simply go somewhere else. With this in mind, I would suggest to you to use images that are smaller in size. This does not mean turn a one inch by one inch image into a ½ inch by ½ inch image. The size of the image in megabytes is what I am referring to here. There are many online websites that will allow you to optimize an image as well as several image editing software programs out there. The trick here is not to optimize an image to the point that it is blurry or looks awful. Find the happy medium.

Emphasis on text is important this is due to the fact that search engine robots do not read images other than to recognize that it is an image so if you are linking to another page within your site that cute little button you found or made will not work as well as a text link when it comes to your search engine optimization! Another thing to keep in mind when designing your page is the use of flash animations. The same rule applies to flash that applies to images: search engines do not read the content of a flash animation they merely recognize that there is a flash animation on the page. If you were planning to build a completely flash designed website you will probably develop a strong hatred for me at this time but the truth of it is that it will not fly with the search engines. Although you can insert your totally flash site into an html page and meta tag the html without content on the page that the search engine robots can read you will have quite a hard road ahead in getting a good listing. Audio files that play on your page as someone gets to your site are also very large files that will slow your load time down. If you are going to use flash or audio then use it sparingly and for heaven's sake do not have it load automatically when someone gets to your page. I am sure you have seen websites with a small media or flash player that you have to click the play button in order for the movie or audio to start. This practice allows the film or sound to load second to the page it's self and the user will not notice a long wait to view the page although the search engine will not be so easily deceived!

The next element of the page that I will bring your attention to is the header tag: <h1>SEO On A Zero Budget</h1>.

We have all seen header tags some of you have seen these tags and not known what they are or even that there is a reason for them so I will try to explain. When we go to a site we may have seen larger text that was above the first paragraph of actual text. In many cases it may have simply said "Welcome" This is usually the case in someone who has built their website from a template an unknowing to the importance of this line thought it was nice to say welcome when someone came to their site! They have just optimized their header tag to welcome along with the 100 million other novice website builders that did not change it. I don't know but if you did a search on any search engine you would probably come up with several hundred million sites coming up for the term welcome! That is a lot of competition for a search term that you do not want to be found under unless maybe you were Welcome Wagon! This header tag will work wonders if you set it to your primary keyword!

Another thing to look at is the alt tag. The alt tag is a tag that should a user not be able to view an image on your site will provide alternate text for the image to the user. Here is an example of an image with an alt tag: <img src="image.jpg" alt="SEO On A Zero Budget" width="738" height="293" border="0" >

Notice that I have instead of describing what the image was I have used my primary keyword. There is a reason for this as I will explain later. Keep in mind that I have set both the header text and the alt tag text to my primary keyword!

 Now let's look at the text on your page. The very first sentence of the very first paragraph on your page should start with guess what? It should be your primary keyword. For those of you are now saying why is he doing this I will summarize it all in a bit and it will be completely clear to you. The first word of the first paragraph can also be bolded and linked to the page that the user is on. This shows the search engine the keyword in bold as well as a text link that is comprised of the keyword. Remember what I said earlier about search engine robots reading text links and not reading images that are linked. This little trick works wonders. The keyword or key phrase should always be used either at the beginning of a sentence or near the beginning of a sentence. This is called prominence; we will explain prominence in the next chapter. Your page should contain 400 to 465 words as a rule in order to achieve optimal success. The page should load quickly and contain a minimal amount of graphics. I am sure we have all at one time or another searched for something and found ourselves on a completely white page with a lot of black text. Not that pretty but we did find it didn't we!

Each page of your site should be designed as described in these pages if you want to realize excellent results and should contain the meta tags described in the previous chapter. Take care to change the meta tags around for each page. A search engine robot will notice immediately that you are using the same meta tags on every page and will not index them all! Any time you can make the keyword or key phrase bold it will be advantages and I suggest it.

Your page must be just as acceptable to the search engine robots as it is to your visitors. Avoid linking off your first or index page to other sites. If a search engine robot finds an outgoing link it looks at as such: If you are getting content or referring to content somewhere else then that content is not on your site and the site you linked to benefits not you. If you must link off your index page then do it with a graphic because as we have already discussed the graphic link is not as relevant as a text link.

FREQUENCY AND PROMINENCE

Prominence and frequency are another very essential part of the way you should design your page. You will want to use your keyword or phrase at the beginning or as close to the beginning of paragraphs and sentences as much as is possible. Also use your keyword or key phrase as much as you can throughout the text on the page. Prominence is where a keyword or key phrase shows up and frequency is how many times it shows up on the page. As a rule your keyword or key phrase should amount to fifteen percent of the text on the page. This may seem like a lot but remember you have used for this example five keywords in your meta tags, spread them out but put your primary keyword or phrase at or near the beginning of as many sentences or paragraphs as possible spreading the other keyword around sparingly. This can be a little tricky at first to write the text on the page where it is acceptable to both the search engine robots and the reader. With a little practice you will learn to write optimized text automatically that both performs and reads well.

As we saw in the previous chapters we used the primary keyword at the beginning of the title, the beginning of the description, the beginning of the keywords, the beginning of the header tag, in the alt tag, then at the beginning of the first paragraph as well the beginning of the first sentence. I hope now that it is clear to you what and why we did what we did previously, prominence. Adding the keywords "frequently" throughout the title, description, keywords, h1 and alt tags should now be a little easier for the novices reading this to grasp. These rules concerning prominence and frequency should not be ignored. They are one of the most important components of a properly optimized page. Following what we have already covered if done correctly will put you well on the way to a top listing on the search engines.

LINKING

We will now explain the practice of linking to you. This is pretty easy to understand. Most search engines especially Google pay a lot of attention to links. You want to have more people linking to your site as opposed to your linking to other sites. Incoming links are beneficial to you and outgoing links are not so beneficial to you. With that said do not go and add a link to your site on every site that allows you to add your link to their database. First of all most of those link farms as I call them will require you to give them your email address and verify that address. The spam will most certainly follow. The other catch can be explained in an easy to understand manner that goes like this: if you have a Google page rank of 4 and you have a lot of links coming in from sites with a lower Google page rank than you it could lower your rank. However if you have a lot of links coming in from higher ranking sites it will bring your rank up. Also when you are linking back to another site, attempt to put the outgoing links on a page other than the first page of your site. Remember that those outgoing links on your index page can be detrimental. One of the keys to a high ranking site is that you have all the valuable information on a particular subject, product or service on your site and the visitor does not have to go somewhere else in order to get that information. The ratio of incoming links to outgoing links on your site is extremely important. Remember good quality links are great; a million low quality links are not.

ADVERTISING

Advertising is essential to your business however it can not only be confusing but it can be expensive as well. As I have titled this book **SEO On A Zero Budget** we will not spend time on paid advertising. I will say that some of the advertising campaigns available can be effective. Advertising on a zero budget is not quite as hard as it seems. Let's look at one very real statistic. Website owners spend millions of dollars for paid advertising on Google in one form or another however 83% of the traffic on Google goes to the first five generic or organic results returned! That should tell you how important those first five spots are. Although Google's paid advertising programs are effective an effective website owner can save his business quite a lot of money by being in the top five. The exposure you get is fantastic and the price is even better.

Now let's go over a few ways to massively increase that exposure on a zero budget. It is safely said that how much free exposure is equal to how much time you wish to put into it. With that being said be prepared to spend a few hours a week knocking out some ads.

If you are offering a product for sale a good thing to start with is Google's shopping. Thousands of online shoppers are using it to find products every day. One other thing I like about it is that it is free to list your product and send visitors to your site. In order to list your product on Google shopping you will need to go to Google and set up a free Google Gmail account as this login will be used for both email and logging in to the Google merchant area. After creating your Google Gmail account go to the Google home page and click the link that says Business Solutions, then click on the link that says "Merchant Center". You can then sign in with your Gmail account, set up your profile and create a data feed of your product. They have several tutorials on creating a data feed on the site. Create and submit your data feed and your product will be listed on Google Shopping.

Another way to advertise on a zero budget is to create is to create a short video on your product or service. This can be done on Windows using Power point presentation and exporting it as a movie or using Windows Movie Maker. Once you have created your movie (be sure to ad a text link telling people your web address) then up load it to youtube.com, vimeo.com and all the other video sharing sites. When the sites you upload to ask you to fill in the "tag" information use your primary keyword. These video sharing sites are amazing at what kind of traffic they produce.

Social networking sites such as facebook.com can work wonders if done correctly. Set up a fan page on Facebook for your product. Just remember the key to Facebook is to keep an edge. An edge is strong when you constantly add comments to the page as well as status updates. Try to add comments that people will answer as when they answer it adds to your edge.

You can also send out press releases on your products from any one of a number of online sites that offer to send out free press releases for you. The more you continue to do this the more exposure your site will get.

RELEVANCE

Finally I would like to mention and explain relevance to you. This is a concept that I have seen an awful lot of people forget. Relevance may seem like rocket science to some however it is very simple to understand. When a search engine robot comes to your website it will compare the title tag, keyword tag, description tag, h1 tag and the frequency and prominence of your primary keyword. It will also check to see if the keywords you have used are actually on the page or "relevant" to the page. I have seen people struggle with this although it is simple to do. It is so simple I will give you a simple explanation of the process: Make sure every single word you use in your title, description, keywords and h1 tags appear on the page. This includes filler words like the, it, and etc.

ABOUT THE AUTHOR

Dr. Glenn Blake PhD. has spoken around the world teaching on the subjects of internet marketing, success and wealth building and branding. He has also written numerous magazine articles, and books and audio CDs and DVDs based on internet principles and success building as well as having starred in two feature films and a documentary based on the subject of success as an internet pioneer. Glenn has also served as vice president of a national utility company as well as being CEO of a technology company he founded. He has constantly been able to place hundreds of websites into top search engine positions. To date he has written produced and directed two feature films and presently speaks on the principles of Quantum Attitude.

INFORMATION

For more information on other Quantum
Attitude titles visit us online at
www.quantum-attitude.com